A POET'S
DIARY

A POET'S DIARY

Lisa Michelle Middleton

ARPress
45 Dan Road Suite 5
Canton MA 02021

Hotline: 1(888) 821-0229
Fax: 1(508) 545-7580

Ordering Information:
Quantity sales. Special discounts are available on quantity purchases by corporations, associations, and others. For details, contact the publisher at the address above.

Printed in the United States of America.
ISBN-13:   Paperback   979-8-89676-232-4
              eBook   979-8-89676-233-1

Library of Congress Control Number: 2024925208

CONTENTS

The Book of Sorrow. 1

    Lady Loneliness. 2

    Sister Sorrow 3

    Shadowy Nightmare 4

    Once Again. 5

    My Only Wish 6

    Labyrinth 7

    Your Silhouette 8

    Inspiration. 9

The Book of Fear 10

    Something I'm Afraid to Show 11

    A Silvery Summer's Dream 12

    The Silvery Song of The Smile. 13

    Floods of Deep Blue 14

    Discontent 15

    The Air 16

The Book of Desire 17

    Just A Hopeless Romantic. 18

    Nobody To You. 19

Scarlet Haze 20

The Childish Poet's Mind 21

Phantom 22

The Kiss 23

My Secret Wish 24

Don't Turn Away 26

The Book of Pride **27**

Storm of Sorrow 28

The Beckoning Horizon 29

Broken Rose 30

Ask of Me 31

Drip 32

Instead 33

To The Serpent 34

What You Meant 35

The Book of Courage **36**

A Sea of Ebony 37

Phantom Ship 38

Farewell 39

A Hellish Maze 40

Here We Are 41

Words of Scarlet 42

The Book of Volition **43**

A Promise 44

A Vow 45

Sacred Ink 46

My View of You 47

Let Me Paint You. 48

Pandora. 49

The Book of Reason. **50**

It Seems So Real 51

In The Woods 52

An Ornament and a Stain 54

Aroma. 56

The Ditch 57

Promises 58

The Book of Love. **59**

The Lighthouse 60

Eternity. 61

The Train. 63

A Love Professed 64

Words in Red 65

Take Me 67

To You. 68

The Blue Within Your Eyes 69

Due North 70

The Book of Truth **71**

Dancing Autumn Leaves 72

The Rainbow of Life 74

Silver Shore 75

Rusty Gate 76

Birth 77

The Jay and Daffodil 78

The Eternal 79

The Book of Sorrow

Lady Loneliness
Sister Sorrow
Shadowy Nightmare
Once Again
My Only Wish
Labyrinth
Your Silhouette
Inspiration

Lady Loneliness

Loneliness has her ways of overcoming people
She silently creeps into your mind and holds on tight
You never know when she will find you there, just standing
All alone and so afraid inside with fear and fright

She found me many times in that exact condition
Where I couldn't help but run into her open arms
Yet somehow, I freed myself and continued living
Knowing that her comfort never did me any harm

So here I am again so full of pain and sadness
Remembering how much she helped all those lonely times
And now I see her standing there and softly saying
"Little girl. I'll help you through. Just close your eyes and cry."

Sister Sorrow

Send me your regard, sister Sorrow
Your presents of sadness and of pain
For my future doesn't look so bright tomorrow
And my purpose seems to be all in vain

Yes, I need your hands to hold me closely
To put tears into the corners of my eyes
The pain is building up somewhere inside me
In the deepest, darkest corner of my mind

I understand the job of sister Sorrow
And I know the pay isn't something worth to show
Because you see, like me, I do not like her
She's a person whom I do not wish to know

Shadowy Nightmare

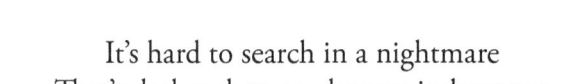

It's hard to search in a nightmare
That's darker than an ebony windowpane
Where eyes of ivory white hold hypnotizing stares
And trap you in an incandescent daze

The blinding darkness never ceases to beckon me
From this shadowy dream I seldom awake
Only once have I reached the edge of reality
To where you stood at the edge of a silvery lake

Reality slipped in only for a moment
A search for a taste almost to an end
When to my surprise the claws of time were sent
To drag me to that nightmare once again

Once Again

I know I've felt this way before
My head is down and my eyes are sore
The sky's the same fond gray envisioned
As when the world kept my soul imprisoned
For I've found that certain skip eludes my step
And the life has died within my breath
That each star is proof of my worthless existence
And each day brings forth newly found resistance
And I realize I'm once again alone

My Only Wish

Midnight has come and gone away
Time slowly moves toward the dawning day
Yet I appear awake

I wish I could find some sleep
But instead, my mind stays up to weep
And time just will not wait
For it feeds upon such a sleepless fate

And I, I stare into the night
I toss and turn in sheets of asylum white
Just wishing I was home
Each memory adds to my endless tome

And now, tears fall down my trembling cheeks
For sadness finds all those she seeks
And turns their hearts to stone
My only wish is that in time
She leaves mine
Alone

Labyrinth

Through these clear walls
I can see the world
Smiling in all her grandness
I can see you laughing
Thinking of me
But the walls are solid
And their heights are endless
And they won't let me walk through
To hold your hand
Instead, they twist and turn
And taunt me with your image
And all I can do to find you
Is trace their paths
And run frantically in every direction
For there are so many hallways
And so many darkened corners
That panic overcomes me
And I drive myself insane

Your Silhouette

With my heart, I see you standing there
Yet nothing stirs the air that bathes my skin
In my mind, you wander aimlessly
Fabricating memories of moments together
You appear in my dreams
Dancing in misty clouds of thought
Running your hand across my deepest emotions

Take your time
If you wish, stay for an eternity
Live within the walls of my heart
Drink the tears that roll down my cheek
Feed upon the images I hold of you

Here you will always be welcome
Even if, with my eyes I cannot see
Your silhouette standing before me

Inspiration

Hello lady loneliness, sister sorrow
For a while I was away
But blue eyes have led me back to you
I've finally lost my way
It's been a while since tears have
Touched these cheeks
Since floods have warmed my eyes
It's a comfort to feel alone again
I feel like myself now when I cry
The spirit that wants me everywhere
Has finally lost its vibrant hold
Contentment has slowly slithered in
To find a heart distant and cold
The vibrant blue of the sky is gray
And greens have turned to black
My words again are rich with tears
Inspiration has decided to drag me back

The Book of Fear

Something I'm Afraid to Show
A Silvery Summer's Dream
The Silvery Song of the Smile
Floods of Deep Blue
Discontent
The Air

Something I'm Afraid to Show

What is this I know?
It's something I'm afraid to show
A little fear
I know I'll always find it here

I guess you were right
I know I'll never hold you tight
It's just a lie
It's something I would never try

The fear fills my mind
A thousand times I'd let you find
My broken heart
I know you'd mend every broken part

If only you knew
These feelings that I feel for you
They'll never fade
And the light will never turn to shade

A Silvery Summer's Dream

My distant friend
I know you not
But still I send
These letters of dancing gold
Behold
A time wherein the
Summers roll
Dreams of silver
Pay the toll
Of the gate that divides our lives
A chime
Does dance within
The churning tide
A wake, I find
But never hide
For the wave of summer dances near
It's here
A song within my
Yearning ear
I know not what or
Whom to fear
Except the fate that dances in my soul
I go
Not knowing what the
Dreams may show
Just hoping some day
I will know
Where the dreams may end
With you perhaps
I hope
My friend

The Silvery Song of The Smile

Dancing dreams, why do you make believe?
Reality is where you yearn to be
What is it here you smile to see?
Why, in the clouds, do you live your life?

In time, I will flee from yesterday
Tomorrow is where I yearn to stay
No dancing dream to lead me astray
From this clutching hand of happiness

And yet, I see the stranger's eyes
Burning in the midnight skies
Coals of blackness rolling by
With stars of silver shining in my soul

I know, the stranger has me in a trance
From his eyes, I cannot glance
Silver stars don't cease their dance
But chant in circles churning ever wild

A smile. Is that what I see beyond?
It sends an enchanting silver song
That wakes me from a sleep so long
And brings me to the doors of reality

Floods of Deep Blue

You say that the world isn't ending
But stars are falling in waves
You say that the moon is still shining
But it's hidden within the sky's caves

I stand here defenseless
Crying in floods of deep blue
The great tide is approaching
Be strong for me to cling to

And you say that the daylight is coming
That the horizon is on the way
But I'm still entrapped in the darkness
And everything leads me astray

You say my world isn't ending
Yet all my wishes fell to their grave
I'm weak, yet I'm the strongest
Fear defines the best of the brave

Discontent

I am awake after midnight
While you lay asleep
I write words by the moonlight
As I softly weep
Beside, the clock's ticking
To the pace of your breath
As I write words of wisdom
Pain, life and death

I know you are angry
By the tension you hide
I know I was the cause
From the scorn in your eyes
My heart is still trembling
From your harsh cutting tone
As I cry here beside you
Afraid and alone

I miss that old world of
"How are you?" and "hello"
While I'm stuck in this hell of
"Are you mad?" and "you should know"
For bewilderment is a battle
I seem to lose everyday
I would have been asleep long ago
If I only knew the right words to say

But instead I know the sound
Of my pen's discontent
Will cause you to wonder
About my awakened intent
And thus this crude cycle
Begins all anew
As I punish myself with
Should haves, don'ts and dos
I don't know how to help
Except to say I love you

The Air

It's funny how no one knows
About my deeply troubled soul
I see the world patiently pass me by
As I sit by my waiting-window and cry
To them I'm only a fleeting face of youth
I carry no importance, faith or truth
I'm here and I'm lost and I don't know why
There is no arrow pointing here
Within the midnight sky
What would they do if I just disappeared?
Is that something this world has ever feared?
Would my mind be missed nearly as much
As my smile, embrace and sweet tender touch?
It's tempting to think of letting it all go
And see what the river Styx has to show
Orion's belt may never house me there
I would only need to stop the air
Stop the air
Just stop the air
… I wouldn't

The Book of Desire

Just a Hopeless Romantic
Nobody to You
Scarlet Haze
The Childish Poet's Mind
Phantom
The Kiss
My Secret Wish
Don't Turn Away

Just A Hopeless Romantic

Each night I sit and daydream
Beyond the starry sky
Say, won't you hold my hand
And wipe the tears from my eyes?
I'm just in a fantasy
At the end of a rainbow
Do you want to meet me there
Beside the silver water's flow?
Love songs fill my hopeless head
As I glide across a glass ballroom
Do you wish to join me dancing
To this imaginary tune?
My head is in the clouds
Drifting past a memory of you
Say, I'll follow 'till the line stops
Or where your love takes me to
And my eyes sparkle when I see you
More than the stars in the sky
'Cause I'm a hopeless romantic
And you're the reason why

Nobody To You

I see you across the hallways
We barely meet each other's eyes
You brush against my shoulder
As you gently pass me by

Do you ever notice me?
Do I ever catch your eyes?
Am I a brighter star
Than the others in your sky?

'Cause my mind goes in circles
When I see your handsome face
And my heart beats faster
In an "I'm in love" unsteady pace

And it's all quite normal
At least in my point of view
'Cause you're a handsome stranger
And I'm just a nobody to you

Scarlet Haze

What is this I feel inside?
Creeping slowly on my mind
Swirls of fire and flames ablaze
A scarlet, violent haze

It creeps upon my broken heart
From where my sorrow will depart
It grows like an ill disease
Like raging, wave-less seas

It grasps onto my falling tears
Of all the hurt throughout the years
Memories of silver shining
Behind a frameless lining

It casts the shadow from my soul
A blinding glare of burning coal
A furnace of desire alights
Before a starless night

The Childish Poet's Mind

The clouds never dance across the sky
Without you passing through my mind
In circles of reddish golden dew
These lonely eyes of hazel brown have chosen you

The birds never sing within the trees
Without you appearing in my dreams
In swirls of jade and marbled white
This childish poet's mind thinks of you tonight

This heart of mine is fixed upon your handsome face
Say, this poem I've made is the only map you have to trace
And each and every day I only wish for you to know
These feelings of mine I'm sometimes afraid to show

A poem never follows the pattern of a rhyme
Without your voice repeating in my head a thousand times
And a song never dances in sync with an enchanting tune
Without my eyes looking for a path to you

This heart of mine is fixed upon your intriguing eyes
Say, my love for you I know I will never deny
I hope that eventually you'll find out who I am
And by then you'll have the compassion to understand
That my heart is only waiting to see
If the love I feel for you, you also feel for me

Phantom

I fell in love with a shadowed light
A phantom dark as a starless night
His eyes glow like a deep black hole
Drawing in slowly my soul

I try to run, but it's no use
The pull's so strong. I can't refuse
There's no way from his churning wake
Turning 'round, there's no escape

While caught, I hear a melody
A distant sound that sets me free
And as I search, I find him afar
Playing a phantom guitar

Each time he strums, the skyline blares
Enchanted notes storm through the air
And when I smile, he starts to sing
Dancing on his guitar strings

And when he plays, it's rock and roll
The only music made for my soul
My broken heart begins to mend
Wishing it would never end

The Kiss

The uncertain fervent glance
The temptress with her golden eyes
And hypnotizing trance
His world disappears
All eyes affixed on ruby cheeks
And grins akin to Tantalus
A knee shakes; fingers tremble
A scent of sweet perfume and soft cologne
Entangle in the evening air
Both minds drift ahead
Thoughts of pouting lips
Dancing through their heads
Knowing just one taste
Would send their hearts ablaze
His pulse becomes a drum
A hundred beats become the song
Of passion's endless rising sun
She steps into his air
The surge of their curiosity oscillates
And their eyes finally meet
With a blinding ferocious flare
A pause of reflection
And a fleeting minute
Feels like a thousand lonely years
And then she smiles
All inhibitions fade like morning dew at noon
And her hand meets his chest
She leans in and inhales his ever-tempting breath
An inch is all that's left
They close their eyes
And before any thoughts can formulate
Or any plans of action set in place
Their lips connect
And they are finally whole

My Secret Wish

I'd walk a million miles
Under a sun intensely burning
And die a million painful deaths
In a storm hellishly churning
If I knew my endless endeavors
Would make true my only wish
But I am certain
Only one thing
Could grant such a wish as this

And this thing is much more painful
And much more trying
And takes all of my faith, and hope, and patience
It's a clock ticking
Sand softly falling
The earth slowly but surely revolving
Oh time, you're painful
When I am waiting
To hear
"I love you"

I ask myself
Is he staring into my eyes because he loves me?
Or does he only stare because he thinks my face is pretty?
Does our handholding mean he can't let go?
Or does he only hold my hand because it's there to hold?
Does his hand caressing my cheek mean I am his everything?
Or does it mean he loves the feel of his fingers on my skin?
I wish us kissing

And us embracing
Meant to him, "I love you"
Instead of "I love the way it feels to hold you"
Oh time, my heart is aching
And softly praying
To hear
"I love you"

My faith is blinding
My hope undying
My patience in this heart forever residing
The clock is ticking
The sand is falling
The earth is slowly and surely revolving
Oh time, you're endless
But I'll wait forever
To hear
"I love you"

Oh darling
My secret wish
Is not to hear "I love you" but to say, "I love you too"
Oh time, you're relentless
And I know that one-day
We'll both say
"I love you"

Don't Turn Away

My life has had hardships
My life has had trials
I've flown over oceans
I've walked a million miles

I thought I had plans
And the truest of dreams
I thought I'd be seeing
The same sheltered scenes

But the winds grew too fierce
And the thunder too loud
The lightning found shelter
In every fortune I found

I thought I could stay strong
And smile for their sake
But my heart finally found me
And won't allow another break

I've had enough hardships
I've had enough trials
And my heart has decided
Has known for a while

Don't turn away
When I say
To you…

It only wants to see your smile

The Book of Pride

Storm of Sorrow
The Beckoning Horizon
Broken Rose
Ask of Me
Drip
Instead
To the Serpent
What You Meant

Storm of Sorrow

I know it's hard but we'll figure it out
Time may be endless but our time's running out
I say don't worry but I cry at night
All alone

I know my future depends upon me
But voices tell me I have a destiny
I say it's hopeless but I try and fight
To survive

I know it hurts but it's the only way
My path is not here so I know I can't stay
I say I'll make it but I'll die from the pain
In my heart

I know I'm lost in the depths of a game
But I still tell you that I'm not insane
I say I'm honest but I lie to save
My image

I know it's wrong but I have to pretend
Must keep on smiling 'cause that's what you expect
I say I'm happy but I fly in a storm
Of sorrow

The Beckoning Horizon

In the darkest corner of the room
Shunned away and never spoken to
I want to be
Hoping for an opportunity

All this pain emanates from around me
All these tears fall because of others
If only I could run away
To some unknown distant place
Where no one stirs this calm ocean that I float in

Life would be so much easier
If only I played a role
No phantom shadows to whisper hatred in my ear
Or silhouettes to scream in terror of their pain
No love to tear apart this fragile heart

Please just take me home
To that island beyond the sea
Where society does not bind the spirit
Or impede the dancing soul
The horizon beckons me

I just want to be alone

Broken Rose

Darling, the storm clouds have settled in
The raging waves have washed the shore
I've been hanging over a monstrous cliff
And found I can't hold on anymore
My mind's consumed by misery
Endless tears have terrorized my soul
I've found the gate to my success
But fear I haven't fare to pay the toll
And in the mist, you stood a knight
Shield in hand and sword withdrawn
You would've fought any approaching foes
Not knowing they had come and gone
Instead the wind whispered silence
And these crying trees rustled regret
My lips were cold with empty smiles
Thinking feigning them would make me forget
But I realized this oak I thought I was
Fell with every gust of whirling wind
And instead of asking help to enforce the roots
I thought it strong to hold pain in
For stubborn pride keeps me alone
And says I deserve the tears I've cried
It built a wall to ward off weakness
And coaxed me to the outer side
And now I lay there, a broken rose
All strength cast into the silent storms
My hand and heart reach out to you
Please pull me from these deadly thorns

Ask of Me

Ask of me the sun and stars
And every drop of rain
Share with me every laugh and cry
And every ounce of pain

But from my eyes, I'll share no tear
And ask never favor or task
For nothing you want is too big or small
And all mine are too much to ask

And now you sleep, without a care
As I lay awake distraught
Sweet dreams my love, for you I'll stand watch
While your troubles, my troubles are not

Drip

Drip, drip, drip goes the rain
Feeling like I'm worthless once again
Hear the thunder clash and clang and roar
Feeling like I'm less and never more
Drip, drip, drip goes my tears
All the bad things are what I ever hear
See the lightning light up the stormy sky
Feeling like a splinter in your eye
Drip, drip, drip goes the sink
Each droplet a reminder I need to think
I hear each word between the steady leak
A little kindness is all I write to seek

Instead

I hate the clouds that dance
And all the birds that sing
I hate how I make you feel
And regret everything

I hate the thought of morning dew
And all the stars that shine
I hate how I'm a liability
And how I'm a waste of time

I hate how I'm not insane
And how I drive you to the edge
I wish I could make you smile
But I only make you mad instead

To The Serpent

What happened sacred lover?
The lust in your eyes is gone
I'm just another woman now
We've lost our sacred bond
Let's venture to the woods once more
And shiver in the cold
But instead you stay away from me
Even when I'm warm to hold
What happened sacred soul mate?
Were you just mad from the cold blue moon?
And now since it smiles back
Have we lost our sacred tune?
The walls that came tumbling down
On that magical mystic night
Have once again been built up
Only now the ends are out of sight
I thought we had the same intentions
And the same sweet hopes and dreams
But instead I lost you darling
When I gave up everything
You may think that I am fooled by you
But I woke up long ago
I thought you had truly opened up
But it was only all a show
If you want me to be your muse
For a time, I'll play the part
But I'd much rather be without you
And spare my fragile heart
So good day sacred serpent
All our time spent was in vain
I would've been anything to you
But instead I'll just be a name
Just a name

What You Meant

I'm sorry I couldn't tell before
It's obvious to me now
Our days of love are over
And I've decided to take a vow
Don't worry about a flirty glance
Or smiles sent your way
I vow to henceforth leave you alone
And watch all things I say
Affection will never slip my tongue
Nor love spill from my wanting eyes
I'll act as if I couldn't care less
When I sweetly say goodbye
And though it will be painful
I'd rather let you go
I feel I'm unimportant now
And these games are all a show
So I will make it easy
And hide my discontent
I'll no longer spend nights worrying
About mixed messages that you sent
That love wasn't really what you meant
It wasn't what you meant

The Book of Courage

A Sea of Ebony
Phantom Ship
Farewell
A Hellish Maze
Here We Are
Words of Scarlet

A Sea of Ebony

I swam out into a shadowed ocean
The sky was black and overflowed with pain
I was caught in a whirlpool of emotion
Battered down by the lightning rain

The water was black like an evil darkness
An opaqueness that sent shivers through my spine
The waves crashed down with increasing violence
And swept me into a roaring riptide

I drifted ever slower into the distance
Floating within the darkness of the night
Everywhere I looked there stood a hindrance
Everywhere a reason for my fright

Until there stood beyond the broad horizon
A silhouette so pale as the dawning day
Which, so slowly, drew me from the desolation
That has led me down this lost and lonely way

Phantom Ship

Shine upon me silvery darkness
Reach out waters of the shoals
Sink this ship that sails blindly
Desert me to an island home

I sail due course to danger
To storms of blackening rage
Hold me instead true tempest
Tear me from this churning cage

The clouds are black with lightning
The winds are frightening storms
These phantom ships surround me
With accusing eyes of scorn

Send me a wave of transport
That will tear me from this stern
And feed me to that darkness
Where calming waters churn

For from within this open ocean
Do I reach the silvery sea
And escape this ship of nightmares
To find once again reality

Farewell

Farewell phantom ghosts and dreams
Soon I'll be leaving these shadowed scenes
I'll walk the river wild until I find
The gate that holds the key to my mind

Farewell, for how long only fate can tell
The smell of freedom's an enchanted spell
It goes through a dreamer's weary eyes
Until it soars into the wind of sacred skies

Farewell, the forest of life seeks my soul
I see its silver canopy as my real home
Drive away the darkness of the dawning day
Farewell, farewell
I see the sunset sway, sway, sway
I see the sunset sway
It's time to go away
It's time to say…

Farewell

A Hellish Maze

I'm standing in a hell
Devoured by my pain
I'd scream for anyone to help
But I know in hell
All screams would sound the same

That freeing door is within reach
Where just beyond lie heaven's gate
But instead this mystic maze grabs hold
And keeps me here
Where I'm left to forever wait

I'm ruled by hell's ticking clocks
Whose hours torture and tantalize
I know I only need to wait
Before heaven opens the door
And greets me with sweet slate-blue eyes

Here We Are

In a world that seems from afar
Laying under strange exotic stars
And a sun sweetly shining
Have no fear
I'll lead you through those unfamiliar fields
And though the clouds are bound to bring us rain
And not every day will we think the same
Know I'll only hold you closer
And I'll never push you away
I'll bring pleasure instead of pain
And as this new world comes to light
Please realize there's no reason for your fright
That this strange moon still shines at night
And each day brings bluer skies
Each dawn takes doubt from your mind
For my love, I lay my heart on the line
I gamble my soul, my life and my pride
To show you I need you by my side
In this new world of a true paradise
We only need to be patient and wait
Push away doubt and create some faith
So smile at this sweet tender start
I'm here handing you my one fragile heart
And don't worry darling if it ever breaks
Just know it's there for you alone to take
It's a bet I'm more than willing to make
So here please choose to remain
Until this world doesn't seem so strange
And know that 'till then you're not alone
But only each day coming closer to home

Words of Scarlet

You know darling when the stars refuse to shine
And when the sun collapses from the heavenly sky
I'll cast the moonlight into your eyes
And with my love I'll hypnotize
I'll set your heart ablaze in a velvety veil
And cast the wild wind into your silvery sail
I'll set your wandering ship upon the truest trail
And love you more than love entails
Darling, sweetheart, when the tempest draws near
I'll build a force field to fight away fear
I'll build a bridge upon the sturdiest piers
And love you truly through the years
And when the tides turn and my skies are gray
I know you'll come and cast the storm clouds away
You'll let the sun shine on my teary-eyed face
And wipe away any sad or troubled trace
You'll be my fortress when armies attack
Guide me through the forest when I've lost my track
Pull me up when I slip through the cracks
And love me with all the love you have
One of the greatest gifts you continue to give
Is inspire my heart, from outside and within
These words of scarlet will continue to live
From the love we share, show and give

The Book of Volition

A Promise
A Vow
Sacred Ink
My View of You
Let Me Paint You
Pandora

A Promise

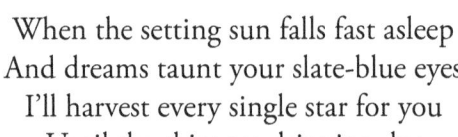

When the setting sun falls fast asleep
And dreams taunt your slate-blue eyes
I'll harvest every single star for you
Until the skies are dripping dry

I'll lay you down on hope and faith
And part your lips with kisses gold
And when your dreams turn gray and weary
Know I'll be there for you to hold

And when you awake to find the sun has too
Don't miss that fantasy where only your mind pays toll
But cling to this wonderful waking world
That conquers the greater heart and soul

For love does not manifest in dreams
But rather in all we do and say
I'll love you with every word and touch
Until infinity finds its final day

A Vow

It's been thrice two moons since our hearts have met
Time enough for them to mend and intertwine
Enough for each of us to know
What lies beneath each other's eyes
Our souls have danced to countless songs
Our minds consumed by company
We've grown to be not two in love
But one in loving unity
With this, I vow now and everyday
To love you with my every breath
And even when the sands of time are gone
And bring age and death of flesh
I vow to wait at heaven's gate
And search for you both near and far
I'll love you with pure heart and soul
And whisper your name to every star

Sacred Ink

The sound of silence is a sweet seductive spell
And loneliness spills over
Through each door within this hell
I had heaven in the sound of
Your sweet and soothing voice
But I made a choice
The sound of silence upsets my writhing soul
I thought I found my sacred gate
I thought I paid the toll
But after all was said and all my deeds were done
I found myself alone again
Without air and without sun
Without love
I was, in fact, alone all along
There is nobody sacred here
No secret special song
No knight in shining armor
No warrior with a spear
My only friend was here
It is here
My pen and paper, each verse and dancing dream
This sacred ink bleeding through in perfect harmony
My companions are my words and tears
My ruby reds and blushing blues
They are all experiences
Walking miles in my shoes
And when the sun collapses
From the surly winter sky
I know my poems will be the last
To flash before my eyes
And my dying wish will be not of love
Or one last kiss, but immortality
For my poems to live on after
I find eternal sleep and eternal bliss

My View of You

Darling, don't be sad to know
That you're not my mystic moon
Nor my sweetly setting sun
Know instead that to me
You're the sweet sky they rest upon
And darling, don't regret
That you're not my shining star
Nor any celestial body dancing afar
But instead you are my universe
And the air I need to breathe
Know, to me, you are a strong foundation
And not a sturdy tree
I could say you're a bolt of lightning
Or a gust of whirling wind
But instead you're every jolt of energy
And every bit of air
That bathes my tender skin
And I ask you not to understand
Nor seek logic, sense or truth
But instead have faith and blindly accept
How these eyes of mine
Have grown to view you

Let Me Paint You

Let me paint you
In greens and maroons
And strong slate-blue hues
For you are much more
Than your face in the mirror
I'll paint every smile
And every tear drop too

Your kindness will shine
In each warming sunray
Your strong will in each oak
And each turning tide
I'll paint your compassion
In all the white roses
And faith in the eagles
That soar through the sky

Your dreams I will paint
In each star of heaven
Your ambition in each snowflake
And sweet patch of ice
Our love will reflect in the
Pink and blue sunset
And strengthen with every
Renewing sunrise

Each stroke of my brush
Is each strand of your hair
And holds every color
From scarlet to blue
So smile each time you
Look in the mirror
For this painting reflects
What I see in you

Pandora

You feign the love of flowers
But really love complaints
I've found the road to happiness
But no one else has found the way
It's lonely at that mountaintop
But at least I have a key
It's time to open Pandora's box
We have eternity

The Book of Reason

It Seems So Real
In The Woods
An Ornament and a Stain
Aroma
The Ditch
Promises

It Seems So Real

Time flies
Beyond these starry skies
Hearts break
Beyond these tropical lakes
It's just a dream, a simple scene
Yet it seems so real

Love spreads
Beyond these distant islands
Smiles form
Beyond these tropical storms
It's just an illusion, simple confusion
Yet it seems so real

Eyes gleam
Beyond these flowing streams
Friends leave
Beyond these tropical seas
It's just an apparition, a simple vision
Yet it seems so real

It's just a dream, a simple scene
Yet it seems… it seems so real

In The Woods

I'm sitting here
In the woods
The moon smiling back at me
The stars whispering
A divinity sharing secrets
Of my future and my dreams
This ground is sacred
Just as all the words spoken here
And every innocent glance
Reflects my inner being
And the completion of my soul
Did He bring me here for a reason?
Was this a glimpse of what awaits
When my flesh is of no use,
When my soul is finally freed?
Will it come here after sunset
And await mystic words
And sacred sleep
To once again roam the earth
When the sun awakens?
Will it someday find truth here?
Did it already find truth?
Did a spiritual realm subtly reveal itself
In the alliance of the trees,
In the significance of every rock
And every lonely leaf?
I am but a single entity

Yet the wind passes through me
And the sun heals my wounds
I am found in every star
Just as every star
Reflects through my eyes into yours
There exists an alarming clarity
And vitality in the woods
I realize this union is beyond all things tangible
And all things physical
Our kisses lay in every word
Our embraces in every glance
Our desires in every tangent of dreamy thought
We have only sojourned here
And yet the essence of my soul remains
To eternally dance with that of yours
And if he decides it's time
That the earth has fulfilled its purpose
And seventy times seven is revealed
May he recreate this spot in the woods
So that our souls may meet again
And linger for all eternity

An Ornament and a Stain

I saw no innocence in him
No naiveté, no hope
Just a blackened, scarred soul
He saw a woman in me
A woman of weakness
Of discontent, of inherent evil
An ornament and a stain on his complicated wall
But a night of chance occurred
And I saw him smile and he understood my mind
We shared sacred words, confessed sacred fears
And for once were not lonely
So we ventured to the woods
Into a blackness darker
Than the hole in his tortured soul
And with every step I saw his soul open up
With every gust of freezing wind
His heart instead unfroze
And the deeper into the woods we hiked
And the more lost we became
The more we found purpose
We found a clearing
And there we cuddled for warmth
There he was capable of affection
Of desire, of happiness
And as that culmination inched closer
And as he almost saw something more in me
The sun arose

And every ray of light brought piercing clarity
And knowledge of life's cruelty
And destroyed all our innocence
And in this growing light
We departed from that sacred clearing
Not knowing we left our souls behind
And each step took us back to pain and suffering
Each step in turn brought another brick
To our sheltering walls
And we lost each other
And now, we walk this earth as shells
For our souls remain
Dancing in the sacred woods
And I see no innocence in him
And all he sees in me
Is an ornament and a stain
On his complicated wall

Aroma

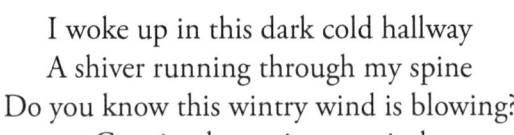

I woke up in this dark cold hallway
A shiver running through my spine
Do you know this wintry wind is blowing?
Creating havoc in my mind

The air is still with death's aroma
But moves now with life's sweet vibrant breath
Let me sit awhile and recite these poems
Before this silence brings forth the air of death

The Ditch

You say you hate to toil
And slave under the sun
But I'd rather work the soil
And have something made when done
You say sweat is for the poor man
And does not afflict the rich
But I admire the tired and sore man
And would rather dig a ditch

Promises

If I spend one more waking moment
In this suffocating place
I fear I'll lose my purpose
And leave without a trace
The air is surely poisoned
The ground paved all around
I desire a redwood curtain
And a songbird's soothing sound
But behold I am afflicted
With a heart that truly cares
And must give up these addictions
For more troubling affairs
I promised love to the lonely
And my time to family too
My money to tax and shelter
And my spirit to all of you
So I say of my endeavors
If I should seem distant for awhile
It is because I keep my promises
And am struggling to feign a smile

The Book of Love

The Lighthouse
Eternity
The Train
A Love Professed
Words in Red
Take Me
To You
The Blue Within Your Eyes
Due North

The Lighthouse

Only time will tell
This enchanted spell
Spills from those eyes
Of perfect golden-honeyed hue
I love you
Been waiting by the riverside
Endless streams slowly floating by
In swirls of the deepest marbled blue
Dance and dream
Let this tempest take your troubles
To that silent stream
The perfect storm
Sends waves crashing against
The perfect weathered shore
But we are warm
We found that lighthouse
Shining through the
Cruel and crashing storm
The fire burns bright
Reflections of vintage wine
Dancing in the pale mystic moonlight
Mountains blue, sandy dunes
Romance spilling from these
Soft enchanting tunes
Hold my hand
Let's run away to that
Distant dreamy land
And give in to the spell
Yes, only time will tell
Only time will tell

Eternity

As far as past and future
I really cannot say
I've found that all predictions
Tend to lose their sense of sway
I'm much too fond of the present
It's something I can feel
Like your smile in the morning
It lives in the realm of what is real

I don't promise to love your memory
Of who you were one yesterday
I don't promise to dream of futures
Where you're more perfect in some way
I love you in the present
When your eyes stare back in mine
I love you in the realm of forever
For right now there is no time

And you needn't say I love you
It's screamed from every cell
And I won't say you are my everything
Because I know that you can tell
For words are hooked on memories
And promises, on what could be
This moment is what I care for
This moment that houses eternity
So let's live in this forever

Where the universe seeks to fuse our souls
Let's love an entire infinity
And pay immortality's only toll
We can find the gates of heaven
If we just forget each dancing dream
And know this fleeting moment
In it's entirety

Let's live eternity
In each thoughtless, countless breath
Let's love to infinity
And escape that dream of death
My gift to you my darling
Cannot be kept, just like the sky
It's that smile creeping upon you
It's that tear in your eye… It is eternity

The Train

My life is a train
On a long, cold drive through
Mountains blue
And sweet waves of grain
Over oceans deep and dark
And ferocious tempests and waves
With countless change
My life is a train

I've been riding to you
Through tropical trees
And mystic mazes
Of purple and cerulean blue
Under sweet clouds of white
And a sun shining through
I'm happy to know
I've been riding to you

I see where the rainbow ends
Where the gold shines through
And snowy banks shimmer
Just around the bend
I see a fire burning bright
And your warming smile
As I sweetly send
My love to you
Where you wait
At the rainbow's end

A Love Professed

Not too long ago
When the world was still human
A man was known successful
By the work he would take pride in
Today with mass production
Where to machines, we pay our toll
A man is called successful
If he can increase his monthly payroll

I understand the favor
For the rich and wealthy taxed man
But I prefer carved redwood table
And will always love the craftsman

Words in Red

They cast your words in red
But your words lived stronger within my head
More subtle and more driving than
A tome that's leather bound

Men used you to promote false pride
They mimicked your pain and remembered your strife
They paid attention to your death, not life
And said their worship was the way

But these mortals are lost in then and what's to come
They think of you as a virgin's son
The put burdens on you of a thousand tons
When there is no burden on us at all

Instead, I honored you as you were on that hill
Your mountain scrmon is what I chosc to fill
The emptiness that almost surely killed
My own uncertain happiness

You said the path was hard to find
You said few tread that sacred line
I thought it a riddle of some kind
But you said just what you meant

I found you, myself, in the lost library
In the old scrolls, I found you in secrecy
You laid the pathway to eternity
And my own everlasting life

Now I hear you say "be perfect just like Him"
Where they say they are too full of sin,
I know our only origin is one unified within
We need only open our eyes

They cast your words in red
But despite my faith, I chose to know instead
And from those words, found the narrow path that led
To that heaven in my mind

To my savior, I love you
You showed me that nowhere without time

Take Me

Take me to the mountains
With snowy slope
And blanketed treetop
A clearing awaits
Let's fuse our souls in passion
And tease amongst the trees
Take me to the cabin
With frosted window pane
And white-trimmed rooftop
A fireplace awaits
Let's share some sweet champagne
And whisper in the air
Love me into the morning
Where even when the sun awakens
I'm still fighting for a breath
An eternity awaits
And the sunrise holds our heaven
So bring me to the mountains
To the lone secluded cabin
And take me

To You

It seems the sun has found me
Before the moon could take my soul
I lost my way to treasure
But found my way to home

With love I have been ignorant
And thought I had the real
But with you I found my heaven
And know now how love should feel

A kiss should be with passion
And one should never turn away
An embrace should shock the spirit
And leave nothing left to say

Nights should swim in passion
And mornings in dreamy dew
For the sun now shines vermilion
And the sky, the deepest blue

Each breath remains reminder
Of what life has left in store
Sweetheart, with your life past is perfect
But life present,
Leaves me hungering for more

The Blue Within Your Eyes

I could say I love you
Like the sun loves the flower
But the sun just isn't bright enough
And flowers fade with the hours

I could say I love you
Like the sailor loves the sea
But the ocean just isn't deep enough
And sailors aren't as free

I could say I love you
Like the stars have loved the sky
But most stars are gone and faded
And the sky
Just isn't the same blue
As that hue
Within your eyes

Due North

If the moon could speak to heaven
Orion would melt away
I've told the moon about you
At dawn and dusk each day

The sun has blushed in envy
Each time I confess a sacred kiss
For he knows his fire and fury
Is no match to passion like this

The stars have laughed like children
When I share each sincere smile
They say they haven't seen me this happy
In the longest moonlight mile

For the rain now waits with lightning
For our love to tempt the thunder
She says to challenge the tempest
And let these feelings take us under

For to drown in sea is frightening
But this sea holds scarlet shoals
And the moon, the stars, and tempest
Have promised to sail our sinking ship
Due north to snowy home

The Book of Truth

Dancing Autumn Leaves
The Rainbow of Life
Silver Shore
Rusty Gate
Birth
The Jay and Daffodil
The Eternal

Dancing Autumn Leaves

Dancing in the breeze
Are the autumn leaves
Of color and delight
The wind then stopped
And I then dropped
At the end of such a sight

I then did stand
As they did land
So fragile on the grass
The wind then blew
And they then flew
They started dancing past

I saw them fly
So way up high
Blending with the light
They disappeared
As I had feared
They drifted out of sight

I looked afar
And saw a star
Within the darkened sky
A wish I made
And there I stayed
Hoping the leaves were by

I looked away
And heard them say
Among the cooling breeze
That they were there
Within the air
The
Dancing
Autumn
Leaves

The Rainbow of Life

Here comes Crimson,
Dressed in drapes
Loveliness flowing over Hate
Orange approaches,
Mind full of Fear
Yellow is wild, not mellow
When his Courage is near
Green lays active
Upon the passive floor
Sleeping, dreaming
Injured Teal gleaming
Pain soothing all his sores
Turquoise waits stubbornly
Understanding and kind
As the humblest Blue Navy
Strolls proudly behind
Purple is smiling
Joyously whole
As the darkest of Angers
Erupts in his soul
Violet stands sneering,
Jealousy proud
As Life enters slowly
Sweetly and softly
Into
The Chaotic Crowd

Silver Shore

I was lost in an abyss
A chasm dark and deep and dry
It shivered and it shook
And spilled and spewed into the sky
I screamed to no avail
Launched ships without their sails
And waded in the churning tide
And when all hope was lost
And I paid more than life costs
I slipped into a dancing dream
To a place where troubles went away
And sunlight gave birth to day
I found myself upon this silver shore
Awakened by an enlightened roar
Supine upon the velvet sand
When I realized I held in my hand
A single granule; no less, no more
And I smiled
I couldn't ask for more
I wouldn't ask for more

Rusty Gate

I was riding on the river Styx
Drenched in blood and tears
When a voice whispered sweetly from within
"I've come to grant you passage
Through heaven's rusted-over gate
You lived the sound of silence
And found eternal fate."

I saw you on the battlefield
Engulfed by hate and fear
When a vision appeared within a silent dream
A billion sleepers marching through
Hell's bustling back door
They loved the blood of battle
But lost the final war

I saw them gaze in wonder
At Orion's gilded belt
When life spoke to me of men's mistake
"The answer does not lay my dear
In the realm they seek above
They must make haste in every moment
To profess eternal love"

I found Him not in service
Nor in steeple or sepulcher
But in breath and blood that courses through my veins
Seek not your salvation
But your defeat of ignorance
We were born for greater purpose
Than repentance for false sin

Realize we are each our own creator
If we only look within

Birth

I was given a home by the divine
But lost at such endeavor
My concept of eternal time
I lost my choice of forever
I lost my will. I lost my way
Bound to earth, my soul dared not stray
I lost immortality and was left afraid
I slowly lost my life the longer I stayed

The Jay and Daffodil

They say the world is black with pain
But its tears are not seen in any drop of rain
Humanity says we've lost the way
But the sun still brings tomorrow after today

They say more wars are bound to come
But I refuse a life lived on the run
For the awakened have found the final key
Let's listen to their true tales of eternity

For the mountains do not cry out in fear
And the seasons cycle endlessly year after year
A leaf doesn't know such pride or pain
That courses through a selfish vein

For if you ask the jay or daffodil
What life is like upon the hill
A sweet song will come from the shades of trees
And silence will sweep the hill in a summer breeze

For life to them is not of who or why
Nor do they question the purpose of sea or of sky
The sun is not one that circles in endless space
But instead, is the source of warmth upon every face

I say the world is more than a house of death
That it's the source of beauty and everlasting breath
Humanity will see that there is a way
If we only focus on the moment, on the present,
On today

The Eternal

If heartache breaks your soul in two
And your spirit falls from Him
They'll be room for the awakened
If there is no room within the inn

Men and women, heaven, hell and in-between
Our minds alone to make them two
Realize happiness lies within the mean
Where He gently runs through you

He's not Him, but it and all
Each grain of sand and DNA
He's not in the past or future at all
He is now, the eternal, today

www.ingramcontent.com/pod-product-compliance
Lightning Source LLC
Chambersburg PA
CBHW051548120626
46551CB00013B/1426